THE DRUM THAT BEATS
WITHIN US

Also by Mike Bond

Novels

Snow

Assassins

Killing Maine

Saving Paradise

Holy War

House of Jaguar

The Last Savanna

Tibetan Cross

THE DRUM
THAT BEATS
WITHIN US

POEMS BY
MIKE BOND

BIG CITY PRESS   NEW YORK

Big City Press, New York, NY 10014

Published in the United States by Big City Press

LIBRARY OF CONGRESS CATALOGING-IN-PUBLICATION
DATA
Bond, Mike – author
The Drum That Beats Within Us/Mike Bond
p. cm.
ISBN paperback: 978-1-949751-00-0
ISBN ebook: 978-1-949751-01-7
1. Literature and Fiction. 2. Poetry. 3. American. 4. Nature. 5. Love.
6. Death. 7. Native American. 8. Ecology. 9. Spiritual. 10. War
10 9 8 7 6 5 4 3 2 1

Cover and book design by John Lotte
Author photo by © PF Bentley/PFPIX.com

Printed in the United States of America

www.MikeBondBooks.com

In memoriam

Richard Bond

Multa renascentur, quae iam cecidere,
cadentque quae nunc sunt in honore vocabula

"In all our searching, the only thing we've found
that makes the emptiness bearable
is each other."

– CARL SAGAN

Contents

Preface

Rooted in the Heart

Ancient as the human heart, poetry is. Alive and well back when we sat round stone-age campfires chewing mammoth bones and worrying about cave bears.

The moment we began to talk, poetry was born. Maybe even before.

Poetry's in what whales and wolves sing. It's in the excited gabble of the mynahs in the tree outside my window, in the soaring voices of the dolphins in the waves offshore. Sharing experience in a memorable way so everyone can learn.

Every clan needs stories, lessons from the past, reliquaries of time. Sitting round our paleolithic fires we shared the day's experiences – antelopes loping over a hill, the muskrat caught, new berries in the next valley, the paw prints of a cave lion on the river bank.

These were the day's news, of opportunities and dangers, how we helped each other stay alive. But after the day's news, as the fire turned to coals and the kids snuggled deeper into the bearskins of their elders, the stories from the past came out. How we find meaning in the incomprehensible, beautiful, tragic and sacred mystery of life.

Tales told of our ancestors, of their courage and wisdom which are our template today. Of the earth before us, the animals and plants and the sacredness of each. The beauty of all life, the meaning of time and the cosmos.

To better be remembered, these stories were often told in rhythm and rhyme, the rhythm of the heart and the rhyme of the mind. And until many millennia later when writing was born, rhythm and rhyme were how things were remembered, passed down through thousands of generations in the alchemy of time. Even long after writing was born, rhyme was central to spoken art.

Only in the last century or so has "free" verse evolved. Far easier to write, obviously, it can nonetheless create sudden impact, touch places rhyme cannot.

"Free verse," Robert Frost famously remarked, "is like playing tennis with the net down." But it calls on a different part of the brain, takes away some tools and gives others. More like a dream, and less so.

For anyone who loves poetry, it's fun to do both.

DYING, DYING…

Despite multiple lamentations over its demise, poetry is still alive and well – especially in one of its most ancient forms: lyrics. In recent decades it has even reached new heights of cultural and artistic prominence, and is the backbone of the major music and cultural evolution of the twentieth century:

Rock 'n' roll.

The simple beauty of the blues lyrics of the 1950s soon evolved into the worldwide phenomenon of rock 'n' roll that has dominated our culture ever since, the greatest musical renaissance since the days from Mozart to Chopin.

And rock 'n' roll songs are often poetry, many of them astoundingly beautiful in words as well as music. United with haunting elegant melodies and savage profound musicality that often transports lyrics to new levels of meaning – poetry has never had it so good. Never been heard by billions of people. Never been loved, as some great rock groups are today, by millions of people from every corner of the world.

All this has however not been good news for the poetry professionals, umbilically tied to welfare stipends from politically correct universities and mindless foundations. Their oft-contorted mis-meanings and other obfuscations, their hooligan destruction of rhythm and rhyme, and their juvenile contempt for the wisdom of their audience, are the major reasons why most people don't even read poetry today.

Because poetry is not an intellectual game to be decoded, but an intense perception of the sacred mystery and beauty of life.

Hilariously, at the same time there's been an irrational effort to destroy poetry from within, led by the same intellectual and literary mafia. Poetry, they decided, needs to be upgraded, so that its meanings become indecipherable. And to Hell with the beauty of the spoken word – it's a puerile concept – let's make poetry ugly in the name of something new, as Le Corbusier did to architecture. And we can appoint ourselves the prophets of this revolution. Because even crap has value if it's marketed as new.

Just as the invention of the camera led to abstract art — a way for its practitioners to proclaim their work as more artistic than a photograph — similarly the rise of sound media in the twentieth century led many poetry professionals to make their constipated lines incomprehensible so they could proclaim, as do abstract artists, *You're stupid if you don't get it.*

And ever since professional poets and other literati inadvisably aimed down the wrong end of the barrel at their foot, thus subjecting us to poetry you need a PhD to misunderstand, shares on the international poetry market have continued their tumble to the lows we see today.

MYSTERY OF LIFE

After we've cleared away the mammoth bones and shoved more rocks against the cave entrance to discourage lions, saber-tooth tigers and bears, after the daily news has been updated and each person has recounted her or his own fears and contributions, we turn to the mystery of life.

That's where poetry comes in.

Because like all mysteries, life is ineluctable. We can't describe it. We can't understand it. But we can feel it. And these feelings mixed with what we do understand gives us the best knowledge we have. Although we have become, since leaving our caves, infinitely more intellectually adept, do we understand any better the mystery of life?

What poetry tells is a story that puts us right in it. In the center of it, the survival point. Then it hits us with a poignant truth, slaps that away and hits us with another.

Nothing important in life is learned rationally. What counts is what we learn emotionally. When something hits us emotionally it stays in our experience, as if it had happened directly to us.

NOW AS TO RHYME

Like every artist today, our ancestors wanted their poems remembered. What better way than for them to be told over and over again? To do that you rhyme couplets or alternative lines, making it easier for your tale-teller to remember and repeat them. Because rhyme is mnemonic – a tool for memory.

Soon you got more complicated, to the unbelievable intricacies of the Viking *Hávamál*, Greek theater, Shakespeare, Russian verse, haikus, and a million other magical poems.

But the goal has always been the same: say the truth and make it memorable.

THEN COMES RHYTHM

Probably the greatest reason for rock 'n' roll's overwhelming cultural dominance in recent decades is its throbbing base lines, elegant drums, magnificently complex and beautiful soaring guitars, and driving rhythms that get your heart up and dancing even if you're sitting in your seat.

It all comes down to heartbeat.

Drive the heart faster and up goes the adrenaline. We pay closer attention, it captures us. Takes over our body as well as our mind. Becomes almost erotic in its intensity.

That's rhythm. Mimicking the heart, making it go fast and slow, puts us in the center of the experience.

Wow. That's poetry.

By uniting knowledge with a sudden shock of emotion, a poem takes us out of our lives into a universe of heightened awareness. And like the tales told round our ancestors' fires, brings us closer to life.

Keeps us alive.

GOD AND ALL THAT

The Cheyenne concept of the Great Spirit, or God, does show up occasionally in the following pages, often like an impoverished relative who appears unwanted at a feast. This is just God's latest incarnation – in the past when we were closer to life and less impressed with each other, God had a greater role in our thanks and fears.

To be a believer or an atheist is the same – both depend on faith. But as the Roman poet Horace – quoted in the preceding dedication – once said, anyone who can look up at the stars and not feel the power of God probably cannot feel much at all. Though in these days of polluted and light-drowned skies, few of us can even see the stars.

But often on wild and windy peaks or savage valleys distant from human ken, or far out on a lonely sea, I've been aware that a great power lives within and all around us, and to deny or denigrate it is to only fool ourselves.

WE SHOULD ALL WRITE POETRY

We should all write and read poems; they better our lives.

Reading poems enlarges our personal awareness of life's exuberance, its terrible destiny. To learn in our own lives from the visions of others, from now and the past.

Writing poems is a window into ourselves, standing before a mirror to see who we are.

To connect with the spirit of the world, which is true but always unknown.

STICKING TOGETHER

With deepest thanks to Lawrence Ferlinghetti, Gary Snyder, Richard Brautigan, and Jack Boyce, and to City Lights Books, Bay Area Poets' Coalition, South Dakota Review, the Montana Poetry Society, Niederngasse, and all the other books and journals in the United States and Europe which have previously published these poems.

ENOUGH ALREADY

There's millions of magnificent poems out there in every language, and many fine books and anthologies, and good teachers everywhere. With the magic of the worldwide web we can find lots of them, almost instantly.

Write them yourself.

That's a good start.

THE DRUM THAT BEATS
WITHIN US

LEAVING INDIAN CAVES, MONTANA

Let's have a final smoke in honor of this place
and of the beauty that it shows despite the world's disgrace,
and of the sanctity of life despite its sore abuse,
and of the timelessness of time, the anguish of its use.

Let's cast a final look of love about the yellowed rims
where in the sharp and timbered draws the daylight softly dims,
where silent in the deeper grass the burnished antelope
graze like sage and boulders across a tawny slope.

Time has stolen life from us although life perseveres;
we fall away like waves of stone eroded by our years.
And when each stone has vanished, and as the cliff recedes,
nothing marks its former place, the absence that it feeds.

Our skin – is it the air? Our soles the grass?
Truly is the earth our heart, as from the earth we pass?

GOLDEN GATE BRIDGE

The burden of the days is lifted
from her shoulders; night has sifted
her solace in the sea. Dawn will break
with only memories of her, a lake
from which no river flowed, and bridged
by solitary steel, sharp-ridged
with suffering. At a time
when all was naught, a turn sublime
of the elemental shoulder, from which she slipped
down like a bird, to die
in cold sorrow, beneath an unlit sky.

MAY I MEET YOU THERE

Life is simple
knowing
the right words.

You are
the sun in my life
the joy in my heart
the gem in my soul.

When I met you
twelve thousand six hundred
days ago, I loved you
from the first instant,
the first look and sound
of your voice.

We're all sentenced
to death, you say.
What greater victory
than to love another
far more than oneself.

The days fade like rain,
poisoned like wolves on the prairie,
eagles fall from the sky,
the sea dies
before our eyes.

If anything comes after
the Hell and joy,
may I meet you there.

RUMI

As you said,
dear friend,
a glass of wine
is life,
for I have climbed
a golden cliff
and nearly died there,
then at last light held
a glass of wine
where reflected gleamed
that golden cliff.

HUNGRY MAGPIE

A hungry magpie
is a world
out of order,

when after so much killing
there's nothing left
to die.

The earth barren
as the raw red skin
of Mars,

the seas deadly
as the toxic
skies.

And to think
one little biped
did it all.

FORT BIDWELL

These words are mine.
The pines darkening
in October snow.
The road descending
to an alkali plain,
these few houses.

Wind drives the owl
from his daytime bed,
crystals form
inside the window.
The light of day
is neutral.

Smoke rises
from the store chimney,
but what to bring
in cold-crippled fingers,
what to barter
for a stolen land?

Captain Jack
held back this day
trading lives in lava beds,
till his betrayal.

We keep the wind, the water
frozen in castoff tires,
cinder blocks and tar shingles,
the school
at the road's end.

It is Fort Bidwell
in a closing year,
a Modoc village
against the mountain,
a Plymouth stalled
on the highway.

Modoc, you are gone now.
I beat you out of my heart
with the slow easy thunder
of drums.
The day lies in drifts
across the road.

LAURA

As if a cat
had left these little marks
between your elbow and the shoulder
against the softest inside skin –
each time a single claw
to feed you
the vacuum of its need.

I CHERISH YOU

How much better to say this
than I love you,
the latter's easy, love's one
syllable when cherish is two

And it's fun too, the love
of words, for the best
words can do
is say how we feel,

but the damn trouble is I
love you so much and enjoy every
minute of you and take pleasure in
you and revere you so what the Hell

I should just say it.

EVENING, MARCH

Day rises from the valleys toward the distant darkening cliffs,
to the innocent of verbiage, the swallows and the swifts
who dive with limpid wingbeats toward the river deep below,
that smells of trout and limber pine, of granite sleek, and snow.

A single herdsman treads the path, eyes locked upon the earth,
a fox hangs cold within his grip, its red jaws stiff with mirth –
a laugh at dying life it is, at irony of day,
to gleam so bright, so sure, so swift, and then be snatched away.

The sheep all hunched like boulders in a muddy close-cropped field,
the calves that bawl at evening as the stream with ice is sealed,
the men in lonely houses with their families and fun,
they and the earth that bears them – so soon to be undone.

We think alas in human terms, in hours, years and lives,
while everywhere around us a childless darkness thrives.

DNA

46 years ago
I met you
your fiery eyes, fierce mind,
and beautiful body
I hungered so much
to fill with mine.
Don't know what
you saw in me,
but it was enough,
cherishing each other
all these years,
and down through
ages to come,
worlds of promise and joy
in every instant.

A SIMPLE PRAYER

That life be furthered
that love grow
and pain diminish
that life lengthen
or evolve
forever, lest it
stop.

How could it stop?
Is life not antithesis
to death?
Death came first —
absolute and universal
cold boiling stone
infinite storms
of heat and light
vast conflagrations

where here and there
from clashing atoms
grew an acid
and from that acid
life.
Is life then
just an evolution
of death?

We are still Adam
in his velvet cage,
Eve still hungry
for an answer.
To understand the atom
you must build a bomb;
to understand life
you must destroy it.

When from far across a canyon
we see a sparrow die
we have changed the world forever,
and nothing evermore
can be what it would

That life be furthered
and love grow
that pain diminish,
life lengthen
and evolve forever,
Lest it stop.

HARBOUR

I am reaching toward, my love,
some understanding,
there is your hair
upon my sleeve, no more
than the memory of your leaning
your life toward me,
mixed wine
in a glass with a silver star
on an oaken table,
harbour lights through a dirty window,
it is the fog blowing mist
across the glass and rain
in eucalyptus.

It is the night. Far below
the city of the hills
and sea, the ships
of the harbour. I am reaching
my love
an understanding
of you and me,
a star
in a glass of wine
and eucalyptus
through the long winter rain.

EVERY WHERE

Death is everywhere,

in grass yanked up for a garden,
fish caught gasping, in battered bloody cars,
in wards and havens, cells and woods,
in night, in day, in every breath.

How to understand not being? No more
than fish can air, or a driver see
his own corpse crumpled in the ambulance light,
the blood-stained sheet, the flickering blue night.

Perhaps non-being by its essence
cannot be, is doomed to failure.
But once infinity was cold and dark
and may soon be again.

TUMULT

The tumult of the world
beckons and destroys us

Ravages of sound, ravines
of pure pain, sensual
ecstasies and death.

Exquisite she gasped
arching her back, her throat,
eyes squeezed shut,

a tender sighing biting
of the lower lip
signals Godhead, the gift

that keeps us going.

BUFFALO CALLER

Buffalo Caller, how still your ancient trade,
how warped in soil your empty bones are laid,
although the silent hoofbeats pound yet upon the grass
as if the herds of centuries rolled past.

Once gone how soon you are forgot,
like skulls a farmer turns, seeing not
a glory that was once, intent
on seams of rye in which his years are spent.

So might a Vandal in Perugian fields, surprised
by bones of antique columns, have surmised
that rainwater had carved them, and thus his race
in unversed assurance all history erase.

So do we exhume you, and the beast
who was your prayer, prey, and feast.

ABSAROKA

These words are nothing
against a sky so vast
no thought can harm it.

Listen, Absaroka,
gone is the dawn
of horses, the sunlit hours
of long grass.
The windblown bluebird's song
is soft and lilting now
with understanding,
like an awakening
from pain-racked night.
Time has carried us
into a newer place.
We shall not forsake
or humble it
with reasons.

Listen, Absaroka
the dawn has died
that brought the day
for so long
when each night was bleak
with suffering
and one by one
the horses died
of winter
or wandered
the forgotten plain
where no man
could follow.

We are prisoners of memory.
The mountain in her sweetness
calls me now,
but it is only her call
that remains.
In my mind's eye
she is tall
and stalwart
like a jay's song
ringing from the pine tops
in the first breath
of winter.

Nothing more.
Nothing of this that went before,
the dying, sorrow,
words and hours,
miscreant dreams
driving men like grass
before the wind.

Peace. In the early mornings
along the Niobrara
the robins call
as always,
the willows talk
amid the water
like women washing,
breezes bend the grass
like children running,
trout play across the stones
beneath the sunlight
not knowing of the change,
perhaps, or do they mourn
the buffalo, await
the antelope's step,

the circling eagle,
God's eye, atop the sky?
God assumes a different face
in concert with the times.
I don't know why.
I try so hard
to believe
it's for some reason
that I don't understand.

See, I can sift the wind
for promise,
follow the hour
of the sun, content
to be but for a moment
without past or time,
always in my heart
pretending
that this is and only this
and not that other
which I know is true.

Soldiers, come kill me
at last. I am a remnant
of a dying people
washed across the prairie
by a war
that knows no end.

SORROW

I cannot touch
what hurts me
it will not go away.

FOXY

Where the moon goes
I wander
Your hair is silk
I weave in fingers
        and dreams
My thoughts tales
        within me
woven by your eyes.

Hunter, I carry home my prey
        to you,
touch the skin of your arm
        remembering
blood of antelopes,
the scent of tall grass.

We have driven cars to the tall
        citadels,
walked long prairies in the
        night,
I have had nothing but the touch
        of your arm
and the stars to guide me.

CROW

Crow eases
across the sky
tilting a wing
to slide this way
or that,
easy as a dream.

What does he see?
This battered earth,
houses sterile
as stones,
driveways, streets,
green lawns
bright with poison.

Flying so easy
life so dangerous and hard.
Does he hate
or only scorn us?
Or is he simply waiting
for us to die?

NOTHING

Nothing
will always
be true.

PROVENCE

Sun
stone walls
green leaves
blue sky.
Cool, warm wind
pine and lavender
distant sea.

The soil steeped
in blood
is dry.

JACK

His life
absent of joy
as a stone of thunder,
his eye
on the horizon,
a fox within his cloak.

At his death
an owl rose
with a rabbit
from the headlights
of the highway.
Was this an omen?

A smile
lurked the corners
of his mouth.
Was he sad
that love could be so little
in so much?

Or was he adrift
on foreign seas, his ear
awake for pounding surf,
his own heartbeat
confounding him
until the end?

GREAT SPIRIT

The Great Spirit
comes sometimes as a fly
on your wrist or chairback.
When you see him
your whole world
opens up.

LIKE A MOOSE WE WANDER

Like a moose we wander,
sink noses into meadows,
succulent green and mud,
willow bud and bark,
icy water purling over rock
flakes of mica, bog and blood.

Like the moose we run
from winter, wolves,
and man's assassinations,
love the loveliness of sun
across a stream
against a weary flank

Like the moose we fear
danger in each breath,
hunt the meaning
of the land,
wonder why the river
bends each year
more to the west

Like the moose we are undone
by passion,
a moment's
sure surcease,
or lope lonely and alone
along the edges
without even the meaning
we do not understand.

OLD FOOL

In truth the old fool brings his own recompense:
spittle on the floor, a scuff there, a quip
older than last year's ribs, and out of sense
with all before, a senile mindless slip.

Yet we invite him – he likes the kids
to ride his knee, and in their solemn ears
casts antic prophecy, his rheumy lids
seamed with recall, a calculus of years.

He never does a dish, just nods goodbye,
hugging the youngsters to his dribbled pants;
I worry as he goes how soon he'll die,
surely he's lived beyond what mercy grants.

And so we suffer him. God knows we each
will soon enough be like him, beyond reach.

MOON OF BLACK CHERRIES

Wishing to be more than I am
or other than I am
or being not complete with the living
that is now mine
being afraid that I am not completely
doing what I am
is crazy now
and always was
and always will be
is
such verbs, such verbs as these
where shall I beguile myself to?
words what words make the difference
between being and being not?
corralled by my ideas I have seen a horse
follow me through a field of grass
without stopping to eat because I
held before her nose a handful of dry weeds

everything that I can learn, that humans with our minds
can learn, must first have been unlearned
in the journey from the prairie
to the city
the most advanced of minds
is only best
at doing with a machine the tasks
the heart was once at home with

I feel tired and dissolute
the cries of children arguing distract me
I think of Yellowstone
of grizzlies
and dusk
a famine of the heart

is what we know
not only the prisoners of 2nd Avenue
but also we who bring our city minds
to the grasslands

there are images that pin my heart
to circumstance
unknown,
blood spurts from the past
release me
grandfathers
spirits
ask me what am I doing
with my hands posed before this typewriter this machine
in adoration? no – simply in ineffectiveness

living in smoke, we are haunted by a dream,
by shapes moving through the cloud
painted warriors riding in and out
we would be them we say
we have not even a candle
hungry for truth, any truth
we have no clothes
no horses
and there is no land left
to travel on
there is truly nowhere left
to go –
is this the truth
we seek?

last night I had a dream
I have had so many

I was on my pony
riding north and east
each day was new
the land unending
I could have travelled for
ever

had I wanted

each day grass
        for the pony
water
        cool to drink
game
        to ease my hunger
antelope
and deer
        and bison
and elk
        and all the four
footed creatures
        of this earth
"Where are you going, little one,"
the grandfathers asked me
"I am going to the hills, O Great Ones,

"I am going to the hills, the Black
Hills, to dance with my enemies the Crows,
under the waxing light of the moon,
the Moon of Black Cherries, under the
yellow moon"

for all that has been before shall be again
all that was is now and always will
nothing lies forgotten under the grass
our dead shall be avenged
for the victors die of poison
and our dead, grandfathers, our
ancestors, have feet of grass,
bones of air

skin of clear stream water
with their sharp eyes they watch me.

PAIN

It takes pain to know it:
the thin man's grimace
    of sorrow,
the fat woman yelling
    at her daughter,
the dog with a broken leg
    on the roadside,
the trapped mouse
    and poisoned rat,
the sparrow
    in a cat's claws,
the climber in the instant
    of his fall,
the hungry child with no
    mother
    or father,
the girl kneeling,
    a soldier's pistol
    at her head.

HOMECOMING

As when Ulysses
from his sad prow
beheld awakened
his childhood land,
so do our memories
transport us.

Returning, we find
the past has lost
the present.
It stands alone,
discreet within us,
no longer true.

EVERY GOOD

Every good
intention
hides a spine
of poison.

ESCALANTE CANYON

Wind-frayed cattails
dance
along the river
like men on horseback
riding into battle,
bending forward,
only to be repulsed
and attack again

The sun is hot
this day in May
and all is withered
in the rite of spring
that passed with an
evening's shower
six weeks ago.

Magpies flit
between the cottonwoods
lynx tracks lie
atop the dust
crickets scream
among the wild oats
Stone bones jut
from the river bank.

Time roils down
its sallow stream
past boulders girdled
in dry moss
while slowly
the hawk circles,
anchored.

LYDIA

Premonition of the dawn
kept her awake
from midnight.
Her dreams subsided
to a vacant rest.
The dark was clothed
in old jewels,
necklaced
by a silver serpent,
her hands restless
on the sill
as if to reach
beyond the glass.

The dawn revealed
her silences. Undertakers
removed the night.
A cat howled.
Over a metal bridge
three thousand miles away
a train rattled.

She did not realize
her sorrow.
Her refusal
she took as fear,
the day to her
some sand
on which
the swimmer
of an everlasting depth
was beached.

Covering her small breasts
in the mourning of cloth,
she boiled coffee, prepared
herself for use
by daylight,
stripping from herself
that last inapproachable
understanding
that only dreamers
know.

ALL THIS TIME

All this time,
while the angular woman chooses broccoli at Safeway
and decides to go back to her husband,
and the old man cashes his $279 Social Security check,
and the pilot lands a plane with 310 people who start talking
on their cell phones.

MAYHEM IN THE BONEYARD

The plots are vain in bloom and flint
to celebrate love's interment.
A swallow lights on granite head
and leaves one drop of excrement.

The bones beneath this lichened show
decay in silence, for they know
distress avails not, nor can dread
offset life's final, comic blow.

We toss the graves an askant glance
while off to frolic, rut, and dance,
quick in the look we give our dead –
as if their fate were sole mischance.

The stones will wait, knowing that ignored
is oft the vault where deepest hopes are stored.

CRAZY QUILT

So many scraps —
    a brother dead
    in Vietnam,
    a sister knocked up,
    vanished.
A mother's nicotined
    hoarse desperation,
the long-ago father,
a rusted tricycle
    in a dusty yard.

In Topeka Women's Prison
the days don't go by
    at all —
It's so little, really,
dealing out the same you got,
the gun's punching bark,
the sorrowed horror in the eyes
as someone dies,
a scrap in time
that makes a pattern
best seen from afar.

STAY

Stay with me
Great Spirit,
and may I stay
with Thee.

PARADISE DUCKS

Paradise ducks don't know
about men and steel.
In rainforest rivers
they love
and raise their young,
always paired, the
dark multicolored male
and white-necked female.

Paradise ducks so easily fly,
don't know about airplanes
carrying men halfway
round the world,
shotguns in their baggage,
men who shoot thousands of ducks
for fun,
who have shot ducks in Brazil,
Mongolia, Canada, and now
in the far south
of the South Island
of New Zealand.

Paradise ducks mate for life.
Men don't.
A duck never kills.
Men do.
Ducks love misty dawns
that men sleep through,
flashing rivers and skies
blue as the gun barrels
that the men who love
to kill ducks
look down
before they fire.

THE MIND SEES ITSELF

The mind grows wise
watching itself,
as the earth sees itself
by sending eyes into space.
Imagine yourself another,
then see you.

KATMANDU

I simply want to understand
Your arms in the lamp light
through the window
are pale and long
Your hair has lost its gold
It is brown now
You sleep alone
in your world.

You get up, dress and leave
I leave
the building changes
We do not know each other
there are others
I fold further into my world.
One day I die.

You stir and speak out in your sleep
Your voice is deep like humming wires
soft like moss and warm
like rain.

You get up, dress and leave.
I leave
The building changes.
I do not try to understand.

MEMORIES OF WINTER

Sun across pine boughs
that two days ago
were bent with snow

Buzz of a fly
new in the incandescence
of life

The sky is spring blue
The dog sleeps in the shade
on warm soft earth

MANHATTAN ELEGY

I'd steal my friends' memories
for a dime, publish them
as mine.
Like apples we subsist on soil,
on pulp, ash, shit,
fish, tourmaline, and groat,
but never mind there's always an umbrella
if it rains.

All who die on Manhattan isle
lose their souls at Hell's Gate,
where tides push back the flow
of gravity,
where down below huge
rusting cephalopods clamber over
sunken oil drums from Istanbul,
wire, mud, and flushed-down ticket stubs,

and the burning sun that rose
beyond the sea at Rockaway
casts brief alpenglow on these stone
peaks, this Chrysler, that spiring
lonely Empire; their snow plumes
crown the city. In the hush
of dusk I hear a lowing and the bells
of cattle coming down for night;

the loud eagle leaves its nest
and clatters across the blue Hudson
toward the far
Secaucus plain.
In the villages the lights
are lit;
already the skins from today's hunt
are up and drying;

we squat round our fires
on our heels;
the stars come out between
the mountains, but we,
being versed in them,
do not bother.
We eat, undress
and sleep, are born,
grow old, and die,
in the shelter
of our hills, in this
valley built of our love,
between the wide blue rivers.

SELF PORTRAIT

The portrait
of the artist
is undone.

She stands alone
seeking
the irremediable.

It is raining.
Her hands are wet,
her heart cold

with expectation.
She will do
a life.

MOST EVIL THING

The most tragic thing
humans do
is war,

our greatest joy
is life's
creation.

The most evil
is to call one
the other.

JICARILLA

Brute Mesa
rising from the inescapable dawn,
so many have sought
and perished with thee
in the silence of contempt.

It is not my day but many.
It is not my life.
It is many times and many rivers
leading to thee
across the cactus plain.

Out of the sun there is no light,
only shadow, and the fear of death.
Moon mother, do not cherish me
for I am gone, and solitude
waits across the desert like the rain.

In the beginning there was a child,
then two, then many.
History speaks
with powder in its teeth;
the walls are dust

that once were houses,
and the river is of air
that waits for no one.
There is truly nothing left to see
and nothing to hold on to.

Jicarilla, and the plain
of many houses, dust
the antelope. The vision
and the dream
are dying.

These are parched words,
wanton with sorrow,
the pain of death
that does not move
or speak.

It is evening along the dry wash.
Pebbles from a snake rob the rock
of silence; colors wait
like lizards
to pounce upon the air.

The sky a vatican
of emptiness above the heads
of all too blind to see
except the truth,
that holds no wisdom.

No wisdom but the pain
of passing years, the slow
crucible of change, the rock
becoming sand
then rock again.

People are and not.
Time changes; form and shape
and truth wend in and out.
Above the desert and the light
stands the Mesa.

CRETE SEA-VOYAGING

We shall sail to Crete.
There is sun,
white stone,
the sea,
and Crete the green
rock mountains,
the bed in the hotel
in Iraklion.
We shall make love
on the grassy beach
where donkey drivers
cross the river.

For now there are apples
and fish, the wind
in eucalyptus,
a dirt road
ending with us.

The world is flat and Crete
slipped off the edge
while we were making dinner.
The child has fallen on the dirt road;
see, his foot bleeds
on the floor.

DON'T SPEAK

Don't speak
till spoken to.
The tiger hunts.

MAYA

In your coming the long
grass rippled like lions
running,
heat of the earth danced
hawks rose and fell,
courting, high over
grey clouds that gathered belly up
like stranded whales
in the far shallows
of the hills.

The antlered prey paused
in their grazing by
scrub islands, seeking
the honeyed filament
of your scent

In your passage the silence
of the plains gave
way to the music of the
hills
You are of soil
water
and the bones of
deer
This land drinks its
unending need
of you

In your going
the wind stills, the
kingfisher hunts
dry beds,
the deer know
the grass knows
as do the stars
for you are not
apart
    no more than this
    the sun could hope
    to hide its dying
    from the sea.

ERGO SUM

The myriad conceptions of an oft-defeated life
rankle with aborted dreams and poorly interred strife,
yet eager as a hawk for prey hope rises in the eyes,
to shrivel there in bitter age, unwinged in arid skies.

The little girl who walks to school, her satchel full of dreams,
soon wakes to hunt her daily bread, fulfill her maker's schemes,
while breathless on a cloven peak her consecrated spouse
is chained in raiments like the sun, his heart an empty house.

The child is born in loving scorn,
as roses spawn in perfumed thorn.
Its days will flee; it holds the key
that opens not, unknowingly.

We wander on, and wonder why
we do not live yet so soon die.

ESCAPE

Horses in bare fields
he watches from the edges
under low branches.
In the distance
blue mountains.

The pennies of the dawn
            have rolled
into the sea,
the wattle blooms beside
the water hole
in the hills

Come into this house
It is empty
It is cold only
        because it has been so long
There is no wonder in abandon

Having no senses I am left
with only wishes
and no way to reach them
The dinosaur who wanted
        to love, perhaps
You laugh? I am shy
All my bones are broken
Hence my walk is jagged

Wandering, I found a
bathtub in a field,
lion's toes in tall grass
A tree frog leaped from the
moss inside

Truly here is my home
I shall let my long hair
down
drink from the stream like
        the deer,
forefeet in the water

I have so long been afraid
and have now nothing
to fear but pain itself,
like a man chained broken to
a wall
hearing only the tramp of a
captor's boot
        down the hall

PROLOGUE

These are the wine days
of October
when trees, threshed
of leaves, bow down
in prayer to winter,
when the sun, anguished
like an old hound,
leaves its bed
late, going early,
when the sap of life
is dried and frozen.

Away, night comes,
again and again,
lengthening its stay,
till
far
upon another planet
what eye discerns
a hollow spot of darkness
where once gleamed
a star?

LIBRA

You're a dancer, it's true,
and no doubt your ellipses
have more to do with me
than I would dare to think,
but I have watched you slip
into your own vortex,
quicksilver on the table of night,
more mercury than venus,
farther from my ambient
track, though closer to the core,
more like the dancer closing down
over herself, in pirouette,
all complete
but for the light.

TO THE POETS AMONG US

There are deeper joys than pastoral,
manlier feelings than manliness,
more truth than in your little foot.

Audience does not make the poet,
adulation no token of respect,
nor mimics proof of style.

Buddha would've burned his lines.
Thoreau wrote his half in jest.
Whitman never postured so.

Wolves hunting deer are quick,
know what they want, do not disguise
their envy of swiftness, nor their hunger.

Salmon spawn in tight streams we
fear to cross; they are not deterred
nor lose their way.

Even the lion has something real
to roar about.

If I were a poet I would
watch the animals, respect the grace with which
they execute their knowledge.

I would listen to the wind
and learn the wisdom
of silence.

Touch the earth, come together with the grass
that mats the fields, understand the joy
of emptiness.

A CHILD'S LAUGH

A child's smile,
her laugh,
and the whole world
is new.

TIME IS CONSUMED

Time is consumed
        in small
mouthfuls
Despair wrung out in aspirins
Huddling in the corners
        of our experience
we seek warmth
food is cognitive
as is pleasure
love is the province of trapeze artists
the rest of us eat popcorn
and spit in the aisles

houses provide
shelter
a private corner different
    from the rest
our envies and our joys transported
   by internal
combustion
fingers intertwine forgiving
nothing
even the dark is light
even the light
is dark

It is hard to persevere
despite despair
there is so little reason beyond blind
preference
so occasionally
adhered to,
if we had visions we would
die of them
even dreams are dreamt
in the cool cocoon sanctity
of sleep.

PAINTED HILLS

We've walked the painted hills,
swum star-spangled lakes,
followed the rivers of our past
to the place of no return.

Death is there.
lucid as a butterfly's foot,
patient as a dream,
unseemly as an old woman's fart,
delicious as a rose.

Come here, my children, Death says,
you've grown so old –
come
let me heal you
so you need change no more.

You'll be vibrant as a dancing light,
deep as endless night,
lovely as a time that never was,
silent as the grave.

HOOKER

You were coming
and raised, each time,
your body up to mine;
I felt the bones
at your hip

and remembered
gray bodies
piled at Auschwitz,
their hip bones
pulling out the skin
      like little wings.

NO BETTER WAY

Do what you say
and say what you do,
no better way
could ever be true.

Out of passion in a time
of plenty
Out of want in time of hunger
Out of seeking a way
in no way
Out of singing an empty
song,
let the coldness of life
deliver me
let the warmth of death,
like sugar in a coffee spoon,
teach me
that all is other
than my dream.

Dream, my dreams are roads that men
and women travel
the sun washes their feet
They have taken off their fears and carry them
                                        slung
over one shoulder.
In the heat of day
in the remembrance of each other's death
they lay them down, these burdens,
and walk on.

The highways of the body
cross the heart
the heart beats out its melody
the stars dance to the melody
the stars shift before the vision
as the dream grows in waking
as fear fades before acceptance
as the traveler leaves the highway
to sleep in the fields.

The men the women stop
they plant corn and build houses
and the sparrows of the fields fly into
their windows
break their necks on invisible panes
of glass
and fall to lie invisibly in
tall grass, heads ajar, feet slightly
curled.

This is but a moment of time past
it holds no new wonder no lesson
there are no truths to carry men like
camionettes along the highways of the soul
no places there to stop
and build such dwellings as the body
hungers after.

And we the dreamers soon lie naked
in the naked fields
we break our necks on panes
of invisible worlds that hold us
tightly clasped
like stones inside a mountain
the sun in passing turns us into grass
that sparrows eat;
our heartbeat joins the stars,
the faraway stars in the great fields
                    of night,
leaves in the great dwelling place
                    beyond the sun,
the stars that break on invisible paths
                    of light,
to fall invisibly into dark time,
heads ajar, feet slightly curled.

CONDOLENCE

How is the weather along the Maine coast?
How high the swell, how ardent the breeze?
Do foghorns still burden the dark with their boast,
and rains dance abandoned over the seas?

How passes the hour, too slow or too fast,
are the old rich with love, the younger still wise?
Are lifetimes moments, does each moment last,
are the sea's darkest depths in each person's eyes?

Might I find you still, beneath the dead leaves,
in the hemlock's dark shade or under white pine,
where the resins of age are stilled in the sheaves
shorn from the sunlight as sorrow from wine?

I shall be absent; in a foreign clime
I scorn my will and cloak my care in rime.

MNEMONIC

Sated she was, cold and hungry, death
in her mind like an old scent,
weary running from it, each breath
thinner, the blood already spent.

Fated she was, an old wolf young,
Alone, as we all are, to die,
still hoping for some hidden tongue,
a lie.

Wandering is aimless
From its aimlessness comes
    unexpected experience
From unexpected experience comes
    new awareness
From new awareness comes growth
    of consciousness
From growth of consciousness
    comes a heightened sense of life
From a heightened sense of life
    comes a heightened awareness of death
From a heightened awareness of death
    comes a heightened sense of loss
From a heightened sense of loss
    comes greater sorrow.

ENDEAVOUR INLET

The pattern in a spider web
and in the tree fern holding it
and in the river stones below
and the moss upon them
and how the water curls around them
and the furl of galaxies
far above
are the same,
some call it God
it's simply meaning
and change,
and its
absence
is
nothing.

CHILDREN SCALPED

Children scalped –
women shot through the breast,
we ran frantically
hands raised against
hot speeding metal,
blood, wind, pain and dust
is all
we remember.

Cheyenne
Arapahoe
Miniconjou
Algonquin
Comanche
Kiowa
Ute
Micmac
Paiute
Sioux
Delaware
Apache
Blackfoot –

Name us all,
hundreds of tribes
thousands of clans,
many millions of lives.

Once the earth was round
and full, and the buffalo
grass tasted sweet
and grew high
in warm summer rains,
we could walk forever
toward sunrise or sunset
clean air
no fences
no roads
skies thick
with birds,
clear rivers and streams,
prairies alive
with animals
of every kind.

And evil a dream
from somewhere
in the future.

UNITY

God and the Devil
are one;
only we
mistake them.

NELSON

The seasons would not heal his wants
nor hush his frail asperity;
recluse in all his childhood haunts
he quailed before eternity.

Harsh-eyed he prayed in words unknown
for worlds of promise, free from pain,
where sower turns to what is sown,
in time, beneath the autumn rain.

The seed, he said, to soil reverts,
its passage as a tree forgot;
as our bones break, and all our hurts
so swiftly fly, so soon are not.

Such thoughts destroyed him – pity, too:
for they are no less false than true.

FORESTS OF THE HILLS

The watchword
is peace
that stands before us
like a drum.

In the hills the trees
are windy; here time
changes not;
all is silence.

It is not love
that remains
nor darkness.
Nothing stays

but perseverance,
all else illusion
without consent
or understanding.

In our youth we ran
the hills, hunted the surefooted,
watched the moon rise
out of silence.

Now older, we stand alone
each a capsule
prepared and sent
with no destination

but to remember
the flowers of the plains,
their small intentions
carried by the wind

into the hills
the dark hills
where nothing grew
but trees.

DUETTO

All endeavors to produce
reasonable alternatives
ended in laughter

so at the beginning
he stated his visions
clearly; he was not
to be dismissed

lightly. Nor was she for that
matter; they held hands
in the moonlight.

It was very nice. So he
said. But for something
lacking
it would have been

fine.

WORKING FOR GORE

Distressed
tendons of a bridge apart
the road asunder

Fatigued
by ineffectiveness
a fly against a granite wall

Sorrowed
by the ignorant the credulous
the devious and vicious

Hopeless,
for the battle itself
is a defeat.

MICMAC

There is no other way, Micmac.
You are gone, the forest grown
      above your trails
or turned to freeways;
the sea lion and the sea
      are dead.
No more frail canoes, Micmac,
no more frail canoes.

REACHING FOR

Drunk with pain
reaching for her who slips
just beyond each time
his gaze
she who is there
across the water
a body entered
only to withdraw again
into the room
her hair, her blonde hair,
reaching out almost
he can   almost
reach her

drunk with pain he drives
fist after fist
through windows that block
the night
glass splits apart
in webs
that catch emptiness
between them
that cradle bloody hands
in glass feathers
which fall like frozen water
to the floor

in the morning she is
        making pancakes
        and he
puts in
new glass

SMITH RIVER

The firs descend like soldiers
from ridge to stream unbroken;
water and wind
in the earth's palm,
canyons cup the sky.

An alder leaf,
pinned to damp rock
in midstream
paints a picture
of the whole,
of the River
draining streams,
creeks,
rivulets,
seeps,
and springs.

In the leaf, life flows
from earth to bough,
from stem to edge.
The River flows
from edge to stem,
to branch, to trunk,
to sea.

In the leaf, sun life
flows also as the River,
from edge to stem,
downward and inward
to the earth.
What is the leaf's source:
the sun? the earth?

The River's source
is infinite,
each tiny drainage
forms the earth,
forms the water.
Or is its source
the sky, the rain,
the rain whose source,
the sea, takes life
from the River?

The River teaches
that all things
are the source
of all things,
each of the other
and of itself.

Each tree is source
to the River: holding
water, feeding the rain,
grasping soil
and rock
through which water seeps
slowly, to a channel.

Each tree is source also
to the earth,
passing into soil at death,
feeding the earth
as rain feeds the River
and the trees.

On the ridges the wind
ripples the firs, washes
through the canyons.
From the ridgetop one
view, from the stream
another. The message
is the same.

THE NAUTILUS' SECRET

Life is a form of chemical change.
Three hundred million years between
the nautilus and the hand
that holds it.

Three hundred million years
of light across a moment
of endless space
to the next sentient thing.

Chemicals flow like light
from one life form
to another. Words
cannot describe it.

We try to discern the one
and the multitude. And cannot.

MUSIC FROM THE MOVIE

He walks
He talks
He carries with us his
    sorrow like a sign
    before his eyes,
as in water
he swims, looking
to himself alone

she watches, she
stands also alone, she
perhaps waits,
I do not know
she, as in water, holds
her place, not seeing
any other.

They side by side
alone, he cannot
see, he does not
watch, as she
alone in her memory
of him
sinks, as a doe, leaning
to drink, beneath
the surface.

TIME

The day before tomorrow
will never come, nor
yesterday
and now
is never.

MASON JAR

Moments of love pass
like butterflies in high eucalyptus
in the wind of coming
winter.

They cloud the sky
their cool wings finally
like leaves
upon the grass.

A few the children carry
homeward, to warm
in mason jars by the window
in the sun of coming winter.

FORESTS DARK OF ELM

Forests dark of elm
dim the day,
feed blue leaves
near earth;
phantom children flit
from tree to tree.

Yet children, yet
I, stop
at a wall
pushed up a century ago
against the edge
once
of a field
by a man who
must have loved sun
more than shade.

So the children, so
I, grasp old stones
spattered under elms;
we guard
the clearing beyond;
we watch the yellow
grass, the red rock
from the shelter
of the dark.

OLD BONES

Show me old bones
and I'll show you kingdoms lost
promises forsaken
the rags of fashion
spent
in worms and dust,

Kissed lips
and starry nights looking out
over cities to the sea;
where, dirt,
is your wonder now
and joy
at life's majesty?

IT'S ALWAYS THE TIME

It's always the time it is
even when you sneak up on it
even when you forget
or try to live without it.

It's always the time it is
you see the clock,
it's changed
anew.

It's always time
creeping past, can't stop it.
But that which is
will stop.

It's always
when it stops.

WHERE FISHES SWIM THERE IS WATER

I've never been stoned
                on anything
but you

Walking down the Metro
                you on the steps
toothless Moroccan grin
                "Take dirty
pictures?"

The beaches wash
                jockeys leave
butts in ashtrays
riding off with her into
                no sunset
but the failing of my own
                dim eyes –
Hark the heron blows
                egrets circle and
                descend
her underpants slip down
                revealing
an acre of sand

HOLLY IN THE SUN

It is afternoon.
In the shadow
of a window
robins sing
from sunlit holly.

Today half over,
I remember only
what I did.
Not joy,
for there was none.

The shadow moves
along the tree.
Soon dark will fall,
the empty cold,
and silence.

There will be nothing
to remember. No past
of consequence. No bright moment
standing out
like holly in the sun.

WHERE A FLEA ONCE BIT

Why does the mind
        look at itself?
Does it think
        constantly
to get what it wants?
What does it want?
It wants to survive – why?
It is a tool for self-preservation,
thus favored by evolution.
It scans constantly
        for danger and opportunity
but sometimes gets locked
        in a cycle
        driven by feelings
        by fear or pain
        or hope or desperation.
Then the mind runs round
        in circles
dwells on the anguish
of the past
        the fear of death,
flits from thought to
        thought
by association.
What we perceive we
        store
next to others like it?

Obsessive,
is when the mind runs on
eternally
        about the same things.
        like a dog scratching
        where a flea once bit
        and now the scratching
        causes the itch.

The same pains
  bedevil the mind
  with the same trash of thought
  for decades
  round and round like a windmill
  long after the well
   has dried.
By looking backward
  from a probe in space
we see that pain
  makes us live the same ideas
  without cease,
as if we could dissolve it
by imagining ourselves
  other than we are,
like the advertisements
  urging us
  to become ourselves
  by buying what they sell.

Yet the mind can put it
  all together
Stitch these errant dreams
  into a quilt
  so beautiful to see
and that covers us at night.

TIMES TWO

You knew the place
that never was,
danced the song
never sung,
spoke of what
was never said,
walked the trail
never to be.

Summer falls, and spring
came later; evening rose
on fiery clouds
to proclaim the day,
this young man old
before his time,
a child upon
his death.

THE DRUM THAT BEATS WITHIN US

The drum that beats within us is primitive as stone,
the song of one who fears not death nor years alone,
who seeks the silent hoofbeats within the ancient glade,
and hunts the sorrowed unicorn beneath the laurel's shade.

The drum that beats within us outlasts all sense of time
and limbers to no earthly tune, no transitory rime.
The politic is not its stead, nor earning, nor the wise;
it abides not reason, nor in dimension lies.

In the lodgepole canyons before the day's alive
you hear it in the flicker, the creek stone and the hive,
you know it in the winter wind that licks about the boughs
and sifts the gifts of years and bones the forest floor allows.

The drum that beats within us is steady as the Bear
who sleepless guards the whirling skies around his northern lair;
although we cannot see him in the glitter of the day
we know that he is visible once light is swept away.

As when the buck has bounded from his needled mountain bed,
his footfalls echo through the pines long after he has fled,
so does the drum beat after us, although we travel past
the touch of every star and space, the wish a wish might last.

Mike Bond

First published by Lawrence Ferlinghetti in City Lights Books, Mike Bond is an award-winning poet, critically acclaimed novelist, ecologist, and war and human rights journalist. Based on his own experiences in many dangerous and war-torn regions of the world and in its last wild places, his poems and novels portray the innate hunger of the human heart for good, the intense joys of love, the terror and fury of battle, the sinister conspiracies of dictators, corporations and politicians, and the beauty of the vanishing natural world.